THE OFFICIAL
NEWCASTLE UNITED
ANNUAL 2019

Written by Mark Hannen

Designed by Lucy Boyd

Thanks to Michael Bolam, Stan Gate, Paul Joannou, Rebecca Myles, Rory Mitchinson and Isobel Reid.

A Grange Publication

© 2018. Published by Grange Communications Ltd., Edinburgh, under licence from Newcastle United Football Club. Printed in the EU.

Photographs © Serena Taylor and Getty Images

ISBN 978-1-912595-15-0

WELCOME TO THE OFFICIAL 2019
NEWCASTLE UNITED ANNUAL

Back in the Premier League for the 2017/18 season, the Magpies continued to prosper under manager Rafa Benítez and earned a very respectable 10th place finish. Hopefully the 2018/19 season will also be a very entertaining and exciting campaign. From everyone at the club, thank you for your amazing support. Enjoy the read.

MEMORIES OF 2018

Martin Dúbravka walks out at St. James' Park to make his debut against Manchester United.

An empty changing room awaits the arrival of the players.

Celebrations at King Power Stadium, Leicester.

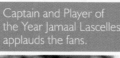

Captain and Player of the Year Jamaal Lascelles applauds the fans.

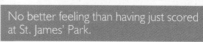

It's all about the team and the supporters.

Almost ready to go…

No better feeling than having just scored at St. James' Park.

Matt Ritchie celebrates with DeAndre Yedlin.

Rafa.

United in the Gallowgate End.

RAFA GUIDES UNITED TO
TOP TEN FINISH

After winning the Championship title on the final day of the 2016/17 season, United approached their 23rd Premier League campaign with a positive outlook. Champions League aspirants Tottenham Hotspur kicked off the season on Tyneside and inflicted an opening day defeat on the Magpies.

But Newcastle bounced back, flying up the table to a heady fourth place come mid-September. That didn't last though, and most of the season was spent in lower mid-table positions until a four-game winning streak in March/April propelled Rafa's side up to tenth spot – a berth they would hold on to for the rest of the campaign and cement with a fine 3-0 win over 2016/17 champions Chelsea at a vibrant St. James' Park.

AUGUST

The Magpies had to wait until Sunday afternoon to kick off their Premier League campaign. They did so in front of the Sky TV cameras, in one of United's 18 live televised matches during the season. Tottenham were in town, but an even contest turned in favour of the visitors early in the second half when Jonjo Shelvey was red-carded after an altercation with Dele Alli, and Mauricio Pochettino's side ran out comfortable 2-0 winners.

Newcastle then made their shortest away trip of the season to face fellow new boys Huddersfield Town, playing in the top flight for the first time since the 1971/72 campaign. The Terriers claimed a single goal victory, leaving the upcoming home game with West Ham billed as a 'must win' – even in August!

Thanks to goals from Joselu, Ciaran Clark and Aleksandar Mitrović, United came up trumps with an emphatic 3-0 success over the Hammers, sending them into the first international break of the season in an upbeat mood.

SEPTEMBER

A long trip to South Wales and the Liberty Stadium was next up for United and their supporters, who made the journey to Swansea City for a Sunday tea-time kick off. Nevertheless, they travelled home in good spirits, after a Jamaal Lascelles header secured a first away success for the Magpies.

A close-run 2-1 home victory over Stoke City followed the next weekend, which lifted United to a season-high position of fourth. The optimism was quickly dashed though, as Brighton – the team Newcastle had pipped to the Championship title just over four months earlier – beat them 1-0 at the Amex in yet another Sunday afternoon fixture.

Still, United were in tenth place and in the early knockings of the season, that wasn't bad. At the top end, Manchester City already had 19 points (out of a possible 21) and were well on course to win the title in what would turn out to be a record-breaking season for the Citizens.

OCTOBER

Liverpool, who were already scoring goals for fun, arrived on Tyneside on the first day of the month and United ended up being satisfied with a point when Joselu equalised – slightly fortuitously – after Philippe Coutinho's rasping strike from all of 25 yards.

Another international break followed before a third long Sunday trek took United to the south coast and the home of the Saints. In a game United should have taken all three points from, they conceded a late penalty which left the Geordies hugely disappointed as they came away from Southampton with a 2-2 draw and a single point.

Crystal Palace, under new manager Roy Hodgson and with only three points on the board were the next visitors at Gallowgate, and this time it was United who struck late on when Mikel Merino headed home with barely five minutes of the contest left.

But October finished in a frustrating fashion, with a 1-0 loss away from home for the third time in five games, this time at Burnley. The Clarets would go on to soar up the table but for United, it was a slip in the opposite direction.

NOVEMBER

November turned out to be a nightmare month for the Magpies, taking just a single point from the 12 on offer. That came at West Brom where United fought back from two goals down to salvage a draw.

Losing at home to Bournemouth was a real sickener, with the visitors heading in their winner in time added on at the end of the game, while the visit of Watford saw the Hornets romp to an easy three-goal victory.

And with Manchester United putting four past Rob Elliot and the Newcastle rearguard at Old Trafford, it was time to regroup and get back on track with the festive period looming.

DECEMBER

A busy month would see Rafa Benítez's men in action seven times, so there was plenty to play for as the New Year approached.

The first four games were lost, including tough away trips to Chelsea and Arsenal, meaning United slipped to 18th in the league. Leicester, meanwhile, won on Tyneside thanks to a very late winner, while Everton's three-point haul was a real smash-and-grab affair.

There was no time for Benítez's charges to feel sorry for themselves though as the pre-Christmas encounter with West Ham – United's first visit to the London Stadium – would be pivotal for both sides. The signs were ominous when the hosts opened the scoring early on, but United roared back with three goals of their own and despite a penalty reply for the Hammers, the black and whites picked up an invaluable three points.

They added another point against Brighton at the end of the month, which preceded defeat against Pep Guardiola's all-conquering Manchester City – although Dwight Gayle nearly salvaged an unlikely draw with a late header, which just went the wrong side of the post.

JANUARY

A New Year's Day trip to the Potteries saw United complete a double over Stoke, with Ayoze Pérez scoring the winner 17 minutes from time. The six points gained against the Potters eventually helped United to mid-table security, while Stoke would be heading out of the Premier League come the end of the season.

In home games against Swansea and Burnley, hopes of a six-point return turned into a paltry two, sandwiching a defeat at the Etihad. But in that clash, United gave the hosts, and champions elect, a real scare when Jacob Murphy made it 2-1 in favour of City with a little over 20 minutes remaining.

FEBRUARY

February started with a good point at Selhurst Park against a revitalised Palace and, considering United had shipped five goals on their last trip to South East London back in November 2016, it was an encouraging start to the month.

And that confidence was taken into the next game at home to Manchester United. Before the game had even kicked off the Magpies had slipped into the relegation zone due to Huddersfield winning, but with Slovakian international keeper Martin Dúbravka playing a starring role on his debut, United clinched a superb 1-0 victory thanks to Matt Ritchie's 65th-minute goal.

Benítez's side wrapped up a good month by drawing 2-2 at Bournemouth, but left Dorset cursing themselves as they had been two-up with only ten minutes remaining.

MARCH

A 2-0 defeat at Anfield got the month off to a bad start with Mo Salah grabbing one of his record-breaking 32 goals, but that set the scene for crunch time, with consecutive home games against fellow strugglers Southampton and Huddersfield on the horizon. Four points was the absolute minimum and six would be ideal.

It turned out to be the latter, with two clean sheets helping the Magpies to two crucial wins. The Saints were clinically dispatched by three goals to nil, with a brace from Chelsea loan signing Kenedy – his first coming after only 64 seconds – and, while Huddersfield proved a tougher nut to crack, Pérez slotted home ten minutes from time following a neat assist from his new Brazilian teammate.

APRIL

When that was followed by a win at Leicester and then Ritchie's winner against Arsenal at a rocking St. James' Park the week after, safety was more or less confirmed with five games still left to play. Four wins on the bounce was music to Benítez's ears and, although United then contrived to lose successive games to Everton and West Brom by a 1-0 scoreline, they still entered the final month of the season looking upwards rather than down.

MAY

A poor first-half showing at Watford contributed to a 2-1 defeat at Vicarage Road before United and their fans made their first visit to the 'new' Wembley to take on Spurs. United lost out to an opportunistic Harry Kane goal, but had many chances to have at least come away with a point.

Newcastle vowed that their four-match losing run would come to an end on the season's final day and it certainly did. The Magpies tore into dethroned champions Chelsea right from the off and their 3-0 win was nothing less than fully deserved on a sunny Tyneside afternoon, when the support from the stands was absolutely phenomenal.

MEDICAL FOCUS

Doctor Paul Catterson oversees the medical department at Newcastle United and it's certainly a very varied role for the Liverpool-born 'Doc' who joined United on a full-time basis back in 2009. Whether it's a 'normal' day at the Training Ground, sorting out a medical for a new signing, or the buzz of a match day, Paul and his colleagues are always on the go. Here Paul talks us through a few pictures that illustrate the highly pressurised, but ultimately rewarding life of one of the most important departments of any football club.

We're starting here with a session in the indoor hall where Jamie Harley, our Head of Sports Science, is supervising a series of early season fitness tests. Pictured with Jamie are Isaac Hayden, Paul Dummett, Jonjo Shelvey and Jacob Murphy. It's vitally important that we obtain data on a player's individual fitness e.g. heart rate, recovery rate, muscle strength etc. so we can monitor them as the season progresses and if necessary, tailor specific training programmes for them.

It's not always glamorous! Here we are on a cold winter's morning just getting ready for training to start. Warm coats and woolly hats are often the order of the day but aside from the staff, it's vitally important the players are protected from the elements and properly warmed up before they begin the more strenuous elements of the training session. We work very hard on that as a team as there's nothing worse than a player 'pulling a muscle' a few minutes into training because he hasn't prepared himself properly ahead of training starting.

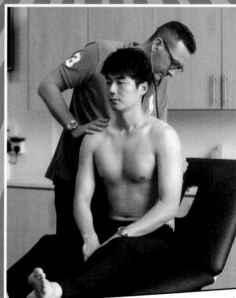

And here I am with Ki Sung-yeung, just before he joined us last July. I'm sure you'll all know that before a player signs for a club he has to undergo a stringent medical examination to ensure that all aspects of his fitness meet the requirements for him to perform at the best of his ability in the Premier League. Here I'm performing an examination before he goes off for an MRI scan which basically scans the muscles and ligaments inside his body. During the season it's quite normal for a player to have a scan just to check the severity of a particular injury, e.g. a hamstring tear.

And that's where Wayne Farrage, one of our sports therapists, comes into the frame. Wayne has been with us since 2012 and his primary role is as a sports soft tissue specialist and Feldenkrais Practitioner, the latter, if you're not aware, is a form of exercise therapy designed to improve body movement. On normal training days Wayne is busiest in the two hours leading up to training when the treatment tables are constantly in use as players, both injured and fit, are having rehabilitation massages or just a general 'getting ready for training' massage respectively. And then when training finishes he's on the go again, primarily relieving any aching muscles from the gruelling session they may have just finished.

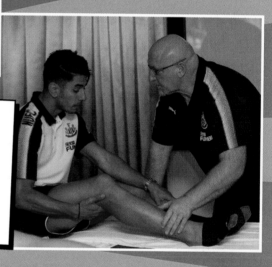

Here's Derek Wright our Head Physiotherapist who unbelievably has been with the club since 1984, so he's seen them all, Gascoigne, Beardsley, Waddle, Keegan, Cole, Shearer etc, etc. He has such a wealth of expertise and experience there's probably no injury he hasn't had to deal with. Derek is pictured here with Ayoze Perez where firstly he has to diagnose the injury and then decide what the best course of treatment is. Sometimes it's just a straightforward strain or pull but when it comes to a player and physio's worst nightmare, for example an anterior cruciate ligament tear (commonly referred to an ACL), well then it's also a case of having to devise a long-term recovery programme, as he had to do a few seasons ago with Ryan Taylor.

And here are myself and Michael attending to Mikel Merino at Arsenal. He'd taken a hefty blow and the two of us just had to make sure he wasn't seriously injured and was fit enough to continue playing. As it happened we made sure he was, after a series of checks, and after leading him off the field, as the rules dictate, he was quickly back into the action.

Michael Harding, our first team physiotherapist, who works alongside Derek, is seen here with myself and other backroom staff on the bench at the Emirates Stadium. We have to be ready at a second's notice if a player needs attention. It's a birds eye view from down by the touchline and a privilege in many ways to be so close to the action. In an ideal world we'll stay put all game!

This picture is actually from April 2016 when Aleksandar Mitrović had suffered a severe bang on the head towards the end of our game with Sunderland at St. James' Park. Aleksandar had just equalised and was desperately keen to get back into action and try and grab a dramatic late winner. However Michael and myself had to look at the bigger picture and when a player's health is at risk, as it was after this incident which caused him to suffer concussion, we had no option but to remove him from the field of play, even though he was desperate himself to return to the fray. It's a difficult one for the player, even the manager, and fans to appreciate but it was 100% the right decision.

WORLD CUP MAGPIES

With the 2018 World Cup having just past, it's undoubtedly the pinnacle of any player's career to play in a World Cup Finals Tournament.

Alan Shearer

Shay Given

Jackie Milburn

And the first Newcastle United player to have that honour was Chilean striker George Robledo who, along with United teammate Jackie Milburn, travelled to Brazil in 1950 for the fourth staging of the world's greatest tournament.

And coincidentally, Robledo's Chile lined up against Milburn's England on 23 June 1950 in the famous Maracanã Stadium in Rio de Janeiro. Robledo played but Milburn was confined to the bench as England won the game 2 – 0. It wasn't until the last group game against Spain, on 2 July, that Milburn played his first game at the Finals.

Robledo also has the distinction of being the first United player to score at the World Cup Finals, firing in Chile's first in their 5 – 2 victory over the USA. And four years later Ivor Broadis scored twice in England's 4-4 draw with Belgium in Basel. Broadis incidentally is United's oldest surviving player (96 in December 2018).

The next Magpie to score was Peter Beardsley against Paraguay in the Mexico World Cup of 1986 (he also scored in the penalty shoot-out defeat by West Germany in Italia 1990 by which time he was a Liverpool player).

Alan Shearer then got England's first against Tunisia in France 1998 and added to his tally against Argentina in the Round of 16 before England agonisingly exited the tournament on penalties, Shearer scoring from the spot in the shootout but fellow Magpie David Batty missed the crucial kick to send the South Americans through.

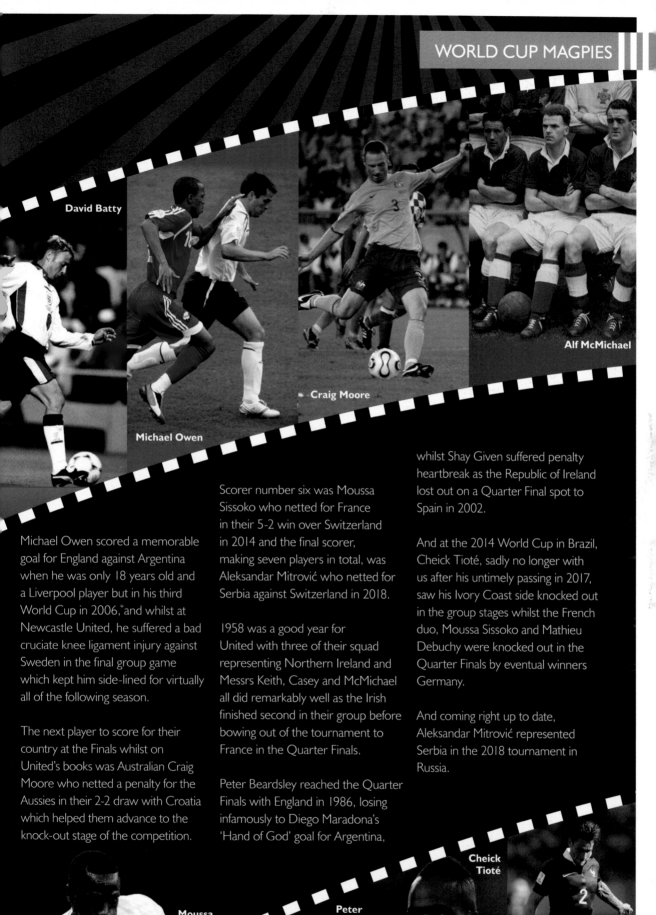

David Batty

Michael Owen

Craig Moore

Alf McMichael

Michael Owen scored a memorable goal for England against Argentina when he was only 18 years old and a Liverpool player but in his third World Cup in 2006, and whilst at Newcastle United, he suffered a bad cruciate knee ligament injury against Sweden in the final group game which kept him side-lined for virtually all of the following season.

The next player to score for their country at the Finals whilst on United's books was Australian Craig Moore who netted a penalty for the Aussies in their 2-2 draw with Croatia which helped them advance to the knock-out stage of the competition.

Scorer number six was Moussa Sissoko who netted for France in their 5-2 win over Switzerland in 2014 and the final scorer, making seven players in total, was Aleksandar Mitrović who netted for Serbia against Switzerland in 2018.

1958 was a good year for United with three of their squad representing Northern Ireland and Messrs Keith, Casey and McMichael all did remarkably well as the Irish finished second in their group before bowing out of the tournament to France in the Quarter Finals.

Peter Beardsley reached the Quarter Finals with England in 1986, losing infamously to Diego Maradona's 'Hand of God' goal for Argentina,

whilst Shay Given suffered penalty heartbreak as the Republic of Ireland lost out on a Quarter Final spot to Spain in 2002.

And at the 2014 World Cup in Brazil, Cheick Tioté, sadly no longer with us after his untimely passing in 2017, saw his Ivory Coast side knocked out in the group stages whilst the French duo, Moussa Sissoko and Mathieu Debuchy were knocked out in the Quarter Finals by eventual winners Germany.

And coming right up to date, Aleksandar Mitrović represented Serbia in the 2018 tournament in Russia.

Moussa Sissoko

Peter Beardsley

Cheick Tioté

Mathieu Debuchy

PLAYERS

The full list of players to have represented their countries in the World Cup Finals whilst playing for Newcastle United is as follows:

George Robledo (Chile)	1950
Jackie Milburn (England)	1950
Ivor Broadis (England)	1954
Tommy Casey (Northern Ireland)	1958
Dick Keith (Northern Ireland)	1958
Alf McMichael (Northern Ireland)	1958
Peter Beardsley (England)	1986
David McCreery (Northern Ireland)	1986
Ian Stewart (Northern Ireland)	1986
Roy Aitken (Scotland)	1990
Alan Shearer (England)	1998
David Batty (England)	1998
Rob Lee (England)	1998
Stephane Guivarc'h (France)	1998
Kieron Dyer (England)	2002
Shay Given (Republic of Ireland)	2002
Michael Owen (England)	2006
Craig Moore (Australia)	2006
Jonás Gutiérrez (Argentina)	2010
Mathieu Debuchy (France)	2014
Moussa Sissoko (France)	2014
Cheick Tiote (Ivory Coast)	2014
Aleksandar Mitrović (Serbia)	2018

MANAGERS

And we mustn't forget the managers! Eight players who went on to fill the St. James' Park hot-seat later in their careers played in the World Cup Finals with two of them, Jackie Charlton and Ossie Ardiles, claiming the ultimate prize, a World Cup winners medal. The full list is:

Bill McGarry (England)	1954
Bobby Robson (England)	1958
Jack Charlton (England)	1966 and 1970
Ruud Gullit (Netherlands)	1990
Kenny Dalglish (Scotland)	1974, 1978 and 1982
Ossie Ardiles (Argentina)	1978 and 1982
Graeme Souness (Scotland)	1978, 1982 and 1986
Kevin Keegan (England)	1982

Ossie Ardiles

Jack Charlton

Rob Lee

Roy Aitken

Kieron Dyer

Jonás Gutierrez

SPOT THE BALL

CAN YOU SPOT THE BALL IN THIS MATCH LAST SEASON BETWEEN NEWCASTLE AND ARSENAL?

AND WHAT ABOUT IN THIS MATCH AGAINST MANCHESTER UNITED?

ANSWERS ON
PAGE
62

PROGRAMME **MONTAGE**

United's match day programme for the 2017/18 season used a different shot of a player for each of the 22 home games throughout the campaign but they were photographs with a difference, each one being taken in a location away from the football field, often chosen by the player himself to reflect his off-field interests.

Hellas Verona – Ciaran Clark at Close House

Tottenham – Isaac Hayden at the Tyne Theatre

Nottingham Forest – Joselu on Tyneside

West Ham United – Rob Elliot at Whitley Bay

Stoke City – Mikel Merino at Kommunity, Newcastle

Liverpool – Jamaal Lascelles in Leazes Park

Crystal Palace – Javier Manquillo on the Quayside

Bournemouth – Florian Lejeune at Housesteads, Roman Wall

Watford – Ayoze Perez at Aveika, Newcastle

Leicester City – Rafa Benitez

Everton – Chancel Mbemba at the Castle Keep

Manchester City – DeAndre Yedlin at home in Newcastle

Brighton – Karl Darlow at Alnwick Garden

Luton Town – Jacob Murphy at Jesmond Dene

Swansea City – Paul Dummett at the barbers

Manchester United – Jonjo Shelvey at Close House

Burnley – Christian Atsu at Hillsong Church

Southampton – Mo Diame at the Titanic Hotel, Liverpool

Huddersfield Town – Martin Dúbravka at Babucho, Newcastle

Arsenal – Dwight Gayle at the La Finca Hotel in Alicante

West Brom – Kenedy in Exhibition Park

Chelsea – Matt Ritchie at home in Northumberland

PLAYER Q&A

MARTIN DÚBRAVKA

Boyhood hero?
Iker Casillas

Best footballing moment?
I have three! Playing Champions League with MŠK Žilina, my international debut and my Newcastle debut v Man Utd

Toughest opponent?
Didier Drogba

Team supported as a boy?
Liverpool

Pre-match meal?
Chicken and rice

Any superstitions?
I don't have any, is that unusual for a footballer?

Favourite current player?
Iker Casillas

Favourite other sports person?
Roger Federer

Favourite stadium other than St. James' Park?
Anfield

What would you be if you weren't a footballer?
An ice hockey player

Where did you go for your 2018 summer holiday?
Bali

What do you like in particular about the city of Newcastle?
The culture and the bridges over the River Tyne

Favourite actor?
Tom Hardy

Favourite TV show?
Friends

Favourite music?
R&B

What do you like doing in your spare time?
Travel

Best friend in football?
Róbert Pich (was with me at MŠK Žilina in Slovakia)

Which three people would you invite round for dinner?
My three best friends

What's the best thing about being a footballer?
Having a job you absolutely love doing

Which boots do you wear?
Nike

What's the best goal you've scored?
I save them!

Favourite football show on TV?
I like Match of the Day

Favourite football commentator/football pundit?
They are all very good

Favourite PS4 or Xbox game?
FIFA

CHRISTIAN ATSU

Boyhood hero?
Abedi Pele

Best footballing moment?
Scoring against Guinea in the 2015 AFCON and winning goal of the tournament

Toughest opponent?
Kyle Walker

Team supported as a boy?
Chelsea

Pre-match meal?
Rice

Any superstitions?
None

Favourite current player?
Lionel Messi

Favourite other sports person?
LeBron James

Favourite stadium other than St. James' Park?
Estádio do Dragão (Porto)

What would you be if you weren't a footballer?
A doctor of medicine

Where did you go for your 2018 summer holiday?
Ghana

What do you like in particular about the city of Newcastle?
The people being so passionate about football

Favourite actor?
Eddie Murphy

Favourite TV show?
Game of the Day on Sky

Favourite music?
Shatta Wale (Ghanaian reggae artist)

What do you like doing in your spare time?
Being with my family

Best friend in football?
Katalin, he's from the Ivory Coast but I played with him at Porto

Which three people would you invite round for dinner?
Lionel Messi, Eddie Murphy and my Mum

What's the best thing about being a footballer?
I just love playing football!

Which boots do you wear?
Adidas

What's the best goal you've scored?
The one against Guinea, but I enjoyed my free kick at Cardiff in April 2017

Favourite football show on TV?
Match of the Day

Favourite football commentator/football pundit?
Alan Shearer

Favourite PS4 or Xbox game?
FIFA

MO DIAMÉ

Boyhood hero?
George Weah and Patrick Vieira

Best footballing moment?
My Senegal debut in 2012 against Cameroon

Toughest opponent?
David Silva

Team supported as a boy?
Paris Saint-Germain

Pre-match meal?
Egg, beans and salmon

Any superstitions?
Looking to the sky and remembering my father before kick-off

Favourite current player?
Cristiano Ronaldo

Favourite other sports person?
LeBron James

Favourite stadium other than St. James' Park?
Old Trafford

What would you be if you weren't a footballer?
No idea, football is my life

Where did you go for your 2018 summer holiday?
Zanzibar

What do you like in particular about the city of Newcastle?
The people live for their club

Favourite actor?
Denzel Washington

Favourite TV show?
Canal Football Club (French TV)

Favourite music?
Hip hop

What do you like doing in your spare time?
I like watching Box Sets

Best friend in football?
I have a lot of good friends

Which three people would you invite round for dinner?
Barack Obama, George Weah and Youssou N'Dour (Senegalese singer)

What's the best thing about being a footballer?
The excitement, the emotion, the pride

Which boots do you wear?
Nike

What's the best goal you've scored?
Maybe the one for Hull against Sheffield Wednesday at Wembley

Favourite football show on TV?
Match of the Day

Favourite football commentator/football pundit?
Thierry Henry

Favourite PS4 or Xbox game?
I don't play

JACOB MURPHY

Boyhood hero?
David Beckham

Best footballing moment?
My goal at Manchester City last season

Toughest opponent?
Ashley Young

Team supported as a boy?
Newcastle

Pre-match meal?
Poached eggs on toast and salmon

Any superstitions?
Left boot, right boot, left shin pad, right shin pad

Favourite current player?
Cristiano Ronaldo

Favourite other sports person?
LeBron James

Favourite stadium other than St. James' Park?
Carrow Road, Norwich

What would you be if you weren't a footballer?
A pot washer

Where did you go for your 2018 summer holiday?
Mykonos

What do you like in particular about the city of Newcastle?
The architecture in the city centre

Favourite actor?
Adam Sandler

Favourite TV show?
Love Island

Favourite music?
Hip hop and R&B

What do you like doing in your spare time?
Sleeping

Best friend in football?
My brother Josh who's now at Cardiff

Which three people would you invite round for dinner?
Anthony Joshua, Cristiano Ronaldo and Kevin Hart

What's the best thing about being a footballer?
That your hobby is also your job

Which boots do you wear?
Under Armour Magnetico

What's the best goal you've scored?
For Norwich against Blackburn, I smashed it in from 25 yards

Favourite football show on TV?
Match of the Day

Favourite football commentator/football pundit?
Rio Ferdinand

Favourite PS4 or Xbox game?
Fortnite

PREMIER LEAGUE
GOALKEEPERS

The position of goalkeeper is one of the key positions in any team, and Newcastle United are no different. Back in February 2018 Martin Dúbravka became the 12th goalkeeper to represent United in the Premier League era (1993-2018) and here we take a look at all 12, listed in alphabetical order, with statistics (Premier League matches only) correct up until the end of the 2017/18 season.

JAK ALNWICK
2016
6 APPEARANCES

Jak was United's third choice keeper during the 2014/15 season but made his Premier League debut in dramatic fashion coming on as a second half substitute for Rob Elliot in the 2 – 1 win over Chelsea at St. James' Park on 6th December 2014 and going on the make seven first team starts over the next month. An excellent shot stopper Jak was schooled at Prudhoe and initially joined Sunderland but moved to Newcastle in 2008. Learnt a lot from brother Ben who has also played in the Football League. Ended the 2017/18 season at Glasgow Rangers after spells with Bradford City and Port Vale.

KARL DARLOW
2015 – 2018
19 APPEARANCES

Karl signed for United from Nottingham Forest in August 2014 but immediately returned to the City Ground on a one year loan. He broke into the Forest team in early 2013 and quickly established himself as the Reds' first-choice keeper. Karl made his Premier League debut at the Hawthorns in December 2015 and was promoted to United's number one in March 2016 when Rob Elliot joined Tim Krul on the sidelines. Karl performed very credibly for United in the final eight games of the season with the highlight being a penalty save from Yohan Cabaye. A key member of the 2016/17 Championship winning team with 34 appearances.

MARTIN DÚBRAVKA
2018
12 APPEARANCES

The 29 year old started his career with hometown club MŠK Žilina, for whom he played six times in the 2010/11 Champions League. He then spent two years in Denmark with Esbjerg fB, before moving to Czech side Slovan Liberec ahead of the 2016/17 campaign. After making 28 appearances for the *Modrobílí*, he joined domestic rivals Sparta in 2017. Dúbravka has been capped 10 times by Slovakia, and played against England in September's 2018 World Cup qualifier at Wembley. Made an outstanding Magpies debut in the 1-0 home win over Manchester United on 11th February 2018.

ROB ELLIOT
2013 – 2018
52 APPEARANCES

Joined United in August 2011, Rob signed his first professional deal with Charlton in 2004 and made 109 appearances for the London side. He also spent time on loan at Bishop's Stortford, Notts County and Accrington Stanley. Facing Southampton in the Premier League on 24th February 2013, Rob completed the notable achievement of playing in the top five divisions of English football. He was called up for the first time by the Republic of Ireland for their World Cup Qualifiers in October 2013 and made his debut against Turkey in 2014. Rob picked up the club's Player of the Year award for 2015/16 and took the number 1 shirt at the start of the 2017/18 season.

SHAY GIVEN
1997 – 2009
354 APPEARANCES

Maybe United's greatest keeper, the former Republic of Ireland international started out at Celtic and joined Newcastle from Blackburn Rovers in July 1997 after loan spells at Swindon and Sunderland. He played in the 1998 FA Cup Final and throughout his time on Tyneside was in a constant battle with Steve Harper to keep the number 1 shirt. In 2001/02 Shay was named in the PFA Premiership team of the season and went to the 2002 World Cup in Japan and South Korea. United's most capped player, winning 82 of his 134 caps on Tyneside, Shay ended his United career on 463 appearances, placing him fourth on the all-time list of games played. Honoured in his hometown of Lifford, Shay was conferred with the Freedom of County Donegal.

STEVE HARPER
1998 – 2013
112 APPEARANCES

United's longest serving player, Steve signed for United from non-league football in 1993 and played in the 1999 FA Cup Final against Manchester United in only his 10th senior match. Prior to that Steve went out on loan to Bradford City, Hartlepool and Huddersfield Town. He played in the Champions League in 2002/03 and saved the penalty at Watford in November 2006 which earned United their first competitive penalty shoot-out win. Took over the undisputed United No 1 jersey when Shay Given left for Manchester City and from the start of the 2009/10 season, Harper, after conceding at West Brom, went 501 minutes without conceding. Also holds the club record for the most clean-sheets in a season (21).

SHAKA HISLOP
1995 – 1998
53 APPEARANCES

Shaka enjoyed a varied 15 year career in England which ended with a FA Cup loser's medal for West Ham in 2005. Standing at six foot four, Shaka was brought up in Diego Martin, Trinidad where one of his friends was famed West Indian batsman Brian Lara. Spotted by a Reading scout he established himself at Elm Park before catching the eye of Kevin Keegan and Newcastle who paid £1.575m for him in 1995. Failing to become first choice, Hislop left United in 1998 on a free transfer, joining West Ham. While on Tyneside, Hislop was active in the Show Racism the Red Card initiative and in 2005 was honoured by the PFA with an award.

MIKE HOOPER
1993 – 1996
25 APPEARANCES

Signed from Liverpool in 1993 for £550,000 to replace the departed Tommy Wright, Mike took over as first-choice goalkeeper initially, but a dip in form saw Pavel Srníček return to the side. Kevin Keegan meanwhile sought to augment his goalkeeper options, firstly with a move for Brad Friedel that stalled over work permit problems and then by signing Shaka Hislop. Hooper meanwhile went on loan to Sunderland in the 1995/96 season but didn't play a game for the Black Cats. Never conforming to the stereotype of footballers, Hooper holds an English Language Degree and is a keen ornithologist.

JOHN KARELSE
1990 – 2003
3 APPEARANCES

Ahead of the 1999/00 season, Newcastle boss Ruud Gullit was looking to boost his goalkeeping options with Steve Harper starting the season between the posts. After just two games – and two defeats – though, Gullit acted to bring in Dutch stopper Karelse from NAC Breda for £750,000. Thrown straight into the mix, big John made his debut at the Dell against Southampton – and let in four goals in 20 minutes after half time. After keeping his place for the following week's 3-3 home draw with Wimbledon, Karelse made way for loan signing Tommy Wright in the Tyne-Wear derby. That was enough to see Gullit depart and following the installation of Bobby Robson as his successor, Karelse made just one more competitive appearance, in a 0-0 draw at Arsenal that October.

PAVEL SRNÍČEK
1993 – 1998 & 2006 – 2007
99 APPEARANCES

One of a small number of players to become a first team regular following a trial, Pav arrived on Tyneside from Baník Ostrava in January 1991. A former soldier, Pav had begun his playing career with army sides Dukla Tabor and Dukla Prague. Becoming a popular figure with fans and players alike, Pav played under both Kevin Keegan and Kenny Dalglish in the following six seasons before his United career drew to a close in 1998 following the arrival of Shay Given but it was a case of "Pavel is a Geordie" again in October 2006 when injuries to Tim Krul, Given and Steve Harper saw boss Glenn Roeder bring Pav back to United where he duly made his 150th league appearance for United. Tragically Pavel died of a heart attack in December 2015.

TOMMY WRIGHT
1993 & 1999
6 APPEARANCES

Only six appearances in the Premier League but 87 games all told for United in two spells at St. James' Park. A highly rated keeper from Linfield, Northern Ireland, he followed in the footsteps of Willie McFaul, United's Fairs Cup winning keeper from 1969, in moving to Tyneside. With fellow custodians like Dave Beasant, Gary Kelly, Martin Thomas and John Burridge around the club, Tommy had to battle hard to earn the right to wear the number one shirt but did so with distinction on many occasions, and one rather infamously in the Tyne-Wear derby monsoon. Led St Johnstone to Scottish FA Cup success as a manager in 2014.

TIM KRUL
2010 – 2017
157 APPEARANCES

Tim joined United from Dutch side Den Haag in July 2005 and was outstanding as United's Juniors reached the semi-finals of the FA Youth Cup. He made his first team debut against Palmero in Sicily on 2nd November 2006, turning in a man of the match performance with regular keepers Shay Given and Steve Harper injured as United won 1-0. After loan spells at Falkirk and Carlisle, Tim made the number one jersey his own in 2011 as he became one of the Premier League's most dependable shot-stoppers. Was part of the Holland squad at the 2014 World Cup in Brazil where he earned hero status in his homeland by saving two Costa Rica penalties in the Quarter Final shoot-out victory.

SPOT THE DIFFERENCE

Can you spot the eight differences in this match between Newcastle and Chelsea?

ANSWERS ON
PAGE
62

27

125TH ANNIVERSARY

The 125th Anniversary of Newcastle United being formed fell during the 2017/18 season and wh[...] United hosted Leicester City at St. James' Park on the 9th December 2017, it marked 125 years o[...] most historic and famous football club. To mark the occasion, the club organised a number of 'ev[...] around the city and we capture them here in a stunning pictorial montage.

The face of legendary 1950s goalscorer and three-time FA Cup winner Jackie Milburn adorns the front wall of the Baltic Centre for Contemporary Art on the Newcastle/Gateshead Quayside. Pictures of other legends such as Alan Shearer, Kevin Keegan, Bob Moncur and manager Rafa Benítez also featured.

The Central Station in Newcastle city centre, a Grade I listed building which was first opened in 1850, is lit up and, in showing its full grandeur, proudly displays the Newcastle United crest on its windows. Hundreds of supporters use the station on matchdays with it being conveniently located just a short walk from St. James' Park.

[...]e iconic Millennium Bridge which spans the [...]ver Tyne and was opened to the public in 2001, [...]it up in celebration of Newcastle United's 125th [...]nniversary. The Baltic Centre for Contemporary [...]t is pictured under its arch.

Outside St. James' Park, an hour before the game kicks off, and the atmosphere is building nicely. Whatever angle or location is used, with the stadium as a [...]

The interior walls of the Level 3 hospitality areas within St. James' Park were completely refurbished with designs and displays illustrating the rich history of Newcastle United. Seen here are Chilean brothers George and Ted Robledo who made a great impact on the field in the early 1950s and on the left, it's a pictorial history of United's club colours from the 1890s.

This shot is taken from the south east corner of the stadium looking across to the giant Milburn and Leazes End stands, always an impressive view.

It's nearing kick off time and supporters all around the stadium are waving their black or white flags, which made a tremendous visual impact, around the whole of St. James' Park. Spine tingling and something you were immensely proud just to be a part of.

The club organised a superb display of flags at the Gallowgate End of the stadium with many heroes from the past being pictorially displayed in the form of huge banners, a fitting and evocative tribute to many of the legends who have graced St. James' Park over the years.

of course it was only right Rafa Benítez was honoured Never since the days of Bobby on have the supporters taken a ger to their hearts as much as have with Rafa.

During the half-time break a host of former United players made their way out on to the pitch having been guests of the club for the day. Around 35 players were in attendance with this picture capturing Darren Peacock, Keith Gillespie, Nikos Dabizas, Pat Howard and Peter Beardsley. The club also named its All-Time Best XI on the day of the anniversary which lined up as follows: Shay Given, David Craig, John Beresford, Philippe Albert, Bob Moncur, Paul Gascoigne, David Ginola, Peter Beardsley, Alan Shearer, Kevin Keegan, Jackie Milburn.

A TIME FOR GAMES

In an age before computers, smartphones and even early television, passing the time of day – away from the football match – was all a bit different for past generations.

Listening to the radio or an old-style gramophone player was the norm, as was reading a good book and the daily newspapers as well as a multitude of table games and even the odd jigsaw. Few of the modern age-band will have ever seen a jigsaw never mind try to complete one – and get utterly frustrated along the way when the odd piece is missing!

In years gone by, many pastimes of this type have been linked to football and we have here two examples featuring the Magpies from the 1930s and 1950s. Scotland

JIMMY SCOULAR

and Chelsea star Alex Jackson – a close colleague and friend of United's Hughie Gallacher – put his name to a series of club jigsaws before the war. The likes of Sammy Weaver, Tommy Pearson and Joe Richardson are part of the 250-piece puzzle (below) whilst a similar United team-group was sold in the Fifties (left).

During pre-war years and introduced in 1929 by William Keeling of Liverpool, the table football game of Newfooty was introduced and became a popular pastime for children and adults alike. Teams could be purchased in your club colours – United included of course. In Tunbridge Wells in 1946, Peter Adolph created Subbuteo and took that concept a huge step forward, with the two rival games competing for a big market. Early Newcastle line-ups were of cardboard

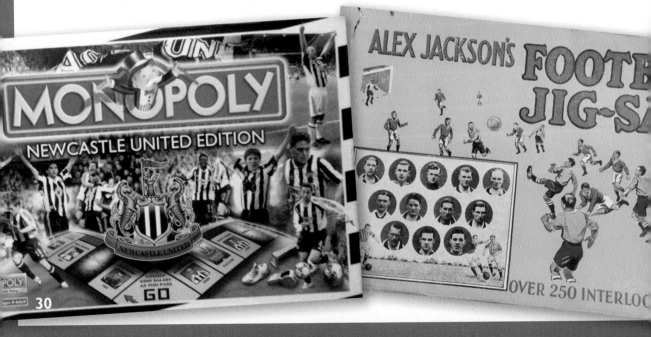

figures but soon plastic statuettes arrived, while in recent years specific Magpies teams could be purchased. The early Newfooty and Subbuteo teams and many accessories are scarce and much collected.

Many card games were retailed featuring football. In the 1920s Piktee produced "League Championship". Later there were games such as "Wembley" and Glaswegian company Pepy's issued "It's a Goal" as well as "International Whist".

Traditional playing cards were also produced, with Monty Gum issuing a wonderful set featuring first-class caricatures of Fifties stars, including Jimmy Scoular, illustrated on the previous page.

Apart from table football, Subbuteo also produced its own card game in the late 1940s and early 1950s, "Soccer Market". Now extremely hard to find and a collector rarity, cards showed various United players.

Board games are not totally a thing of the past. Some are still hugely popular such as Monopoly and Cluedo. And both manufacturers have issued Tyneside editions with a United flavour to them. Monopoly, first unveiled in 1935, also issued specific Magpies versions packed with cards and questions on the Black n' Whites.

The Newcastle & Gateshead edition of Cluedo – "The Classic Mystery Game" originally launched in 1944 – features St. James' Park and notes: "A body has been discovered in the murky waters of the River Tyne, can you solve the crime?" The famous original characters have been replaced with certain Geordie lookalikes; some reckon Professor Plum is a bit like Dec Donnelly, while the Reverend Green has a resemblance to Alan Shearer!

Football card games still exist, too. Subbuteo still produce 'Squads', a colourful set of cards which can be played between two players, there is a quiz game called 'Pride' while 'Top Trumps' and its various football editions can pass the time away between matches. It can be fun to put the laptop or tablet to one side and go back to an almost lost age of cards, table games and jigsaws – all with a hint of Newcastle United.

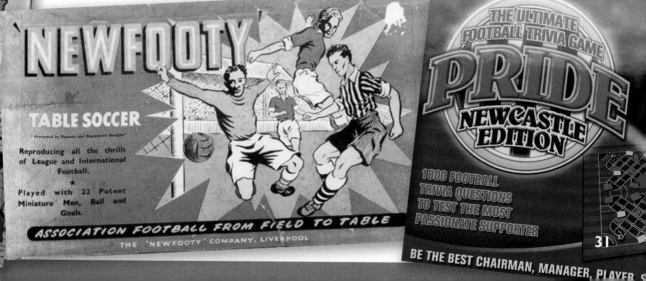

CLASSIC **MATCHES**

We caught up with two former players who gave us their recollections of two outstanding games from back in 2002. Firstly it's Nikos Dabizas who scored the only goal of the game in United's derby day win at the Stadium of Light in February and then Andy Griffin who kick-started our Champions League group stage campaign with a never-to-be-forgotten winner against the mighty Juventus at St. James' Park in October.

SUNDERLAND v NEWCASTLE

PREMIER LEAGUE, 24 FEBRUARY 2002, STADIUM OF LIGHT, 48,290

United travelled to the Stadium of Light third in the Premier League table and with the last two derbies having ended 1 – 1, both teams were looking to break the deadlock. The Magpies were the form team though having won their previous three games and, thanks to Greek defender Nikos Dabizas, United won by the only goal of the game.

Nikos takes up the story:

"We didn't change anything leading up to the game, Bobby (Robson) was clever in that regard and we went into the game very relaxed, just following our normal routine, even though it was a very special game, derbies always are.

"Our mental approach had to be spot on and it was. We started the game well and thought we had the better of things in the first half. It was scoreless though but 20 minutes into the second half, well that's where it really got interesting. Aaron (Hughes) was fouled down the right wing and when Laurent (Robert) swung it in Al (Shearer) got his head to it, the ball

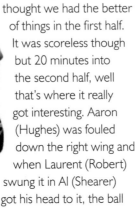

flashing across the six yard box. Sylvain (Distin) and I were both there and I got ahead of him to guide the ball with my head into the net and then all hell let loose.

"I maybe got a bit carried away, ripping off my shirt, but the celebrations in front of our fans were something really special. I'd scored against both Manchester United and Middlesbrough earlier in the season, but this goal was easily the most important. It meant that my name went down in the history books.

"It really is a great feeling when you score the winning goal for your team. But it is even better when you manage to come up with the only goal of the game. Their keeper had already saved one from me with his legs and then I saw my shot hit the woodwork. I was beginning to get a bit frustrated.

"I scored against Manchester United in a game that was seen by millions of people live on television, but this one was even better. We had to hang on a bit at the end but Shay made a world class save from Kevin Phillips to earn us the points."

And a beaming Bobby Robson added:

"It was nice to claim my first victory over Sunderland and my first win at the Stadium of Light. We didn't have a cushion at any stage and we had to show great tenacity and great resolve which won us the day."

United: Given, Hughes, Distin, Dabizas, O'Brien, Speed, Solano, Jenas, Shearer, Bellamy, Robert (Ameobi)

NEWCASTLE v JUVENTUS

CHAMPIONS LEAGUE, 23 OCTOBER 2002, ST. JAMES' PARK, 48,370

United had finished fourth in the Premier League in season 2001/02 and entered the Qualifying Round of the Champions League where they eased past NK Željezničar (Bosnia). Then came the big guns in the Group stage where United lost their first three games to Dynamo Kiev, Feyenoord and Juventus without even scoring a goal! It was time for a revival and when Juve arrived at St. James' Park for the fourth match in the series, things had to change – and they did.

Andy takes up the tale:

"It was win or bust, we knew there was no point in having qualified for the tournament if we were just going to go out with a whimper. We hadn't done badly in the first three games, even though we'd lost them, but we knew what we had to do. It was a challenge we were all up for and even though Juventus rolled in with their superstars, players like Buffon, Thuram, Del Piero, Davids and Nedved, we weren't overawed or daunted by the task, we just couldn't wait to get out on the park and get stuck into them. Bobby wanted us to play with our heads and that's what we did.

"The first half was fairly level and even as the second half progressed we were still confident of grabbing a goal. And then, just after the hour, the stadium erupted.

"We won a free kick near the corner flag down the right and Laurent surprised everyone, including me, by playing it to me as I ran forward. I got clear of their defence and drilled over a cross-shot from close to the by-line. Nobby Solano was in the middle but Buffon just deflected it into his own net.

"IT WAS MY GOAL AND NOBODY WAS GOING TO TAKE IT OFF ME."

"It was my goal and nobody was going to take it off me. There was a little bit of luck involved, and it wasn't the prettiest, but I didn't score many so I was having that one. It was only the second goal I'd scored but unbelievably, like buses coming past, I got another three days later against Charlton!

"This one was easily my most important and although they put us under a bit of pressure towards the end, Harps kept them at bay and we got our first three points on the board. Of course we went on to win the next two games as well which got us out of the group, the first time a team has ever qualified having lost their first three games, something that made us all very proud."

Bobby Robson added:

"That goes down as one of my greatest Newcastle victories, my players showed incredible resolve and tenacity. We must take pride in the fact that we have defeated one of the most powerful teams in Europe and a side which had not tasted defeat this season."

United: Harper, Griffin, Hughes, Bramble, O'Brien, Speed, Solano, Jenas, Shearer, LuaLua (Ameobi), Robert (Viana)

YOU ARE THE REF

EXTRA BALL It is the last minute of injury time at the end of a match, the ball is in the crowd and they refuse to hand it back for the throw in to the opposition. The taker grabs the spare ball from the ball boy, takes the throw in and, just as his team mate heads it in, the original ball is thrown back into the area. What do you do?

SUPER SAVE A goalkeeper seems to make a world class fingertip save and is congratulated by his defenders - he even pumps the air - but as the opposition try to take a quick corner you are convinced that the keeper never actually touched the ball, your linesman isn't sure so what do you decide ?

ONE-ON-ONE A striker is through on goal in a one-on-one with the opposing goalkeeper. He is pulled down but as you blow your whistle and signal for a penalty, you see the ball roll on into the net. What actions do you now take?

EMBARRASSING MOMENT The score stands at 2-2 in the dying seconds of a match and, as a shot comes flying towards your face, well off-target of the goal, you instinctively put your hands up to shield yourself. You are then horrified as the ball flies into the net. What now?

RUGBY TACKLE A long ball forward totally bamboozles the opposing goalkeeper and the ball bounces over his head as he rushes out to intercept it. A defender and two attackers chase after it and the defender rugby tackles the striker in front to the ground. The other attacker is clear though and taps the ball into the net. What is your decision?

PENALTY SHOOTOUT It's a cup game and you are into extra time. The home team's star striker gets injured and can't continue. All the substitutes have been used so the home side has to play on with only ten men. They make it to the penalty shootout and the same star striker wants to take a penalty as he now says he is fit again as the injury has passed. Do you let him?

ANSWERS:

EXTRA BALL If the original ball that is thrown back into the penalty box hasn't interfered with play in your opinion then you award the goal! If, however, the ball has interfered with play, you must disallow the goal. You need to be sure!

SUPER SAVE It is your decision, decide quickly and stick to it regardless of what the players and crowd think. If you think the goalkeeper didn't touch it then award the goal kick and not the corner.

ONE-ON-ONE Firstly, if you have blown the whistle and signalled a penalty then you must stand by that and not award the goal. Ideally, you should have delayed your decision when the incident happened and you could then have allowed the goal by playing the advantage. You should also send off the goalkeeper.

EMBARRASSING MOMENT You have scored the winner, as embarrassing as that may be. You need to calm everyone down and explain that the officials are part of the field of play as are the bar, goalposts and corner flags. The goal must stand!

RUGBY TACKLE Award the goal and then show a yellow card to the defender for unsporting behaviour. You cannot give him a red card as the other attacker obviously had a goal-scoring opportunity so, in effect, the defender didn't deny that goal-scoring opportunity. You correctly played the advantage and the goal was scored.

PENALTY SHOOTOUT No, you do not. Only the players that finished the match may take penalties but what you do have to do is make the numbers even by instructing the other team to remove one of their penalty takers. If the player in question had come back onto the pitch before the final whistle at the end of extra time, he could have

SHEARERRRRR...

Alan Shearer is United's most famous goalscorer. He is also an England legend (30 goals) and now a highly respected BBC football pundit. To many he is United's greatest ever player, a centre-forward who wore the iconic United number nine shirt with distinction bagging a record 206 goals for his boyhood heroes. Here we detail some of Alan's favourite goals, not necessarily the best, but also the most significant, plus a word or two from the man himself on each goal, interspersed with some fascinating off the field pictures.

18 JUNE 1996
England v Holland (Wembley)

Just before he joined United there was the small matter of Euro 96. And on a wonderful balmy night in north-west London, England produced a memorable display to defeat the Dutch 4-1 with Alan and Teddy Sheringham scoring two each.

England were two-up when Paul Gascoigne made a searing burst into the penalty area and when the ball fell to Sheringham he found Alan with a 'no-look' side-foot pass that was hammered past Edwin Van der Sar by England's number nine.

"This was the best performance by an England team I'd ever played in and what an atmosphere it was."
ALAN SHEARER

21 AUGUST 1996
v Wimbledon (H)

This was Alan's home debut and what a way to announce himself. David Batty had given United an early lead but with two minutes remaining, United hadn't wrapped up the points. Not to worry, a free kick awarded to the home side just outside the box at the Leazes End saw Alan curl a superb right-footed shot past a helpless Neil Sullivan. It was a strike of stunning quality and who would have known then there were 205 goals to follow!

"It was nice to get off the mark, and also to seal the three points. You are judged on goals and you have to score them."
ALAN SHEARER

11 APRIL 1999
v Tottenham (at Old Trafford)

3 NOVEMBER 2001
v Aston Villa (H)

This was United's second semi-final in a row at Old Trafford, they scored three goals and our man got them all. The winner against Sheffield United 12 months earlier was followed by a penalty against Spurs early in extra time. With two minutes remaining Alan confirmed another Wembley trip for United with a wonderful strike, latching on to a loose ball on the edge of the area and striking a superlative shot which looped over Ian Walker and just under the crossbar. The goal sent the Spurs fans heading for the exits and the Toon Army into raptures.

> I was happy with the penalty, of course, but the second one is one of my all-time favourite goals, both for the way it went in and the significance of the goal.
> ALAN SHEARER

United were in the top six and were looking to consolidate their lofty position in the table. Five minutes into the second half and one goal to the good, Craig Bellamy attacked down the left before laying it off to Rob Lee who immediately sent a diagonal cross over to the right, where Alan watched it all the way on to his right foot and Peter Schmeichel saw the second volley of the afternoon disappear over his right shoulder. The placement was exquisite and it was the sort of goal that the crowd just had to say 'Wow'.

> It was the look on Schmeichel's face that made this one even more memorable. Rob played the perfect ball for me and I met it just perfectly, caressing it into the net.
> ALAN SHEARER

1 DECEMBER 2002 v Everton (H)

Maybe the best of them all. Trailing 1-0 to Everton with under five minutes left, another hopeful downfield punt found Shola Ameobi's head and, at that point, no-one imagined what would follow. The ball looped up and Alan hit something that Richard Wright in the Everton goal probably didn't even see. Like a howitzer, the ball rocketed into the corner of the Gallowgate goal to send St. James' Park wild.

> This has to be top of the list every time, I have to say I caught it sweet as a nut – and it flew in.
> ALAN SHEARER

11 MARCH 2003
v Internazionale (A)

United were in the second group stages of the Champions League and facing the formidable Italians in their own Milan backyard, backed by over 10,000 travelling Geordie fans. It was 1-1 when Nobby Solano chipped a ball forward for Craig Bellamy to chase down the right. Confronted by two defenders Bellamy skipped away from Guly and slid over a cross for Alan to side-foot home from a couple of yards.

> This was a night that Newcastle United matched one of the finest teams in Europe. The fact that I got two goals simply added to it.
>
> ALAN SHEARER

4 FEBRUARY 2006
v Portsmouth (H)

Alan's record-breaking 201st goal for the club. It began with Shay Given's long kick forward which was met by Alan's header. Shola Ameobi then back-heeled it to the onrushing Shearer who flicked the ball under Dean Kiely with his right boot from eight yards to send the ground delirious with joy.

> It was the best feeling I ever had scoring for Newcastle United and gave me the most pleasure. The ovation from the fans went on for ages and is something I will never forget.
>
> ALAN SHEARER

17 APRIL 2006
v Sunderland (A)

Michael Chopra had just equalised for United at the Stadium of Light when Charles N'Zogbia was tugged to the ground by Justin Hoyte, referee Chris Foy immediately pointing to the spot. In a hostile environment Alan thumped the ball powerfully to the right of Kelvin Davis' despairing dive. The look on Alan's face was just priceless as he stood, arms aloft, in front of his own people.

> My last goal in my last game is a special one. Having missed one against them six years earlier I really wanted to score this one. I knew where I was putting it and in it went. The keeper was never going to save it. There was a lot of frustration and anger in that penalty!
>
> ALAN SHEARER

QUIZ TIME

TEST YOUR KNOWLEDGE ON CURRENT AND OLD MAGPIES!

PRESENT DAY

1) Massadio Haïdara made only one League appearance last season. Who was it against?

2) Which United player made his debut against Huddersfield in March?

3) Who scored United's fastest goal of the season?

4) United were awarded one penalty last season – against whom?

5) Who scored United's last goal of 2017?

6) Against which two teams did United do the double over?

7) United's average league attendance was 49,274, 50,825 or 51,992?

8) Who is United's goalkeeping coach?

9) Which team did Rolando Aarons join on loan in January 2018?

10) Who was the first visiting player to score at St James' Park?

UNITED PAST

1) Which team did United sign Tino Asprilla from?

2) Who was the last United player to score at Wembley?

3) A United keeper from 1976 had a son who played for United from 2006-09. What's their surname?

4) In which year did United win their first FA Cup?

5) How many goals did Andy Cole score in the 1993/94 season?

6) What was the score in the first ever Tyne-Wear derby in 1898?

7) Who has scored the most FA Cup goals for United?

8) Who did United play their very first Football League match against?

9) Who was the last United player to score a hat-trick against Sunderland?

10) Against which lower league team did United field their youngest ever line up in 2009?

ANSWERS ON PAGE 62

CHAMPIONS 1926/27

Was it really over 90 years ago that United last won the Football League Division One (Premier League) title? They've come close since, of course, notably in 1995/96, but never got over the line as they did in April 1927 when a draw at West Ham saw them pick up the point they needed to win the Championship. Here we look back at that memorable campaign.

Captain Hughie Gallacher began his second season on Tyneside having seen the Magpies finish in tenth place the previous year. Taking over the captaincy from the long-serving Frank Hudspeth, United opened their campaign with a resounding 4-0 home victory over Aston Villa with 'Wee Hughie' (he stood only 5'5" tall) grabbing all four goals. The next three games only brought one point as the Magpies slipped to 14th in the table, hardly title-winning form. United didn't lose again until the end of October, a 2-0 reverse at Roker Park, and moved into the top five with a run of three successive wins at the end of November.

Local rivals Sunderland were seen as title rivals that year but it was Huddersfield Town, title winners for the past three seasons, who ran neck and neck with United for most of the campaign.

But what a festive period it turned out to be for the black n' whites. Starting on Christmas Day, with a thumping 5-0 win over Cardiff City, United won six on the bounce to end January in pole position in the table.

With Newcastle, Huddersfield and Sunderland consistently picking up points, the contests with their immediate rivals were decisive as the title race reached fever pitch. Firstly United's Wearside foes were defeated 1-0 at St. James' Park and then a few weeks later, Huddersfield suffered the exact same fate with the winner in both games being scored, of course, by Gallacher. The 67,067 crowd for the Sunderland game established a new record high attendance for United.

They would slip to second on a couple of occasions but after climbing back to the top of the league with a 6-1 Gallowgate victory over Arsenal in early April, they never looked back and maintained their lofty position, clinching the title for the first time in 18 years with two games to spare with a 1-1 draw at West Ham, Stan Seymour netting the vital goal for the Geordies.

Gallacher was the key to United's success netting a record 36 league goals during the season (39 in all competitions) which included five hat-tricks. But it was United's outstanding frontline of Gallacher, McDonald, Urwin and Seymour who rampaged their way through opposition defences which took United to the title, not forgetting of course ever-present keeper Willie Wilson who helped United to the best defensive record in the division that season. Meanwhile the 96 goals scored by United is only second to the club record 98 scored in 1951/52.

And the title-winning Manager? Well, there wasn't one! The team was ran by a Directors Committee, a regular manager, as we're used to these days, not being appointed until 1930.

TOP SIX

	PL	W	D	L	F	A	PTS
Newcastle	42	25	6	11	96	58	56
Huddersfield	42	17	17	8	76	60	51
Sunderland	42	21	7	14	98	70	49
Bolton	42	19	10	13	84	62	48
Burnley	42	19	9	14	91	80	47
West Ham	42	19	8	15	86	70	46

MOST APPEARANCES:

42	Frank Hudspeth, Stan Seymour, Willie Wilson
41	Tom McDonald
39	Tommy Urwin
38	Hughie Gallacher

TOP SCORERS:

36	Hughie Gallacher
18	Stan Seymour
17	Tom McDonald

Stan Seymour

Frank Hudspeth

Tom McDonald

Willie Wilson

COLLECTORS CORNER

Collecting football memorabilia comes in many forms. The most well-known and popular collectables are probably match programmes followed by such items as autographs, badges, books, shirts and other club related paraphernalia.

Less well known items that football loving enthusiasts collect are Royal Mail first day covers which are postage stamps on a cover, postal card or stamped envelope and franked on the first day the issue is authorised for use within the country of the stamp-issuing authority. The covers, rather than marking the issue of a stamp, commemorate events instead. A design on the left side of the envelope explains the event or anniversary being celebrated and sometimes even the stamp or stamps affixed relate to the event.

The postmark is one of the most important features of a cover. Stamps are cancelled by a postmark which shows they have been used and can't be re-used to send the letter.

Newcastle United, throughout their history, have featured on a number of first day covers and we display a number of them below and at top of next page.

The Age of Steam – commemorating the LNER Locomotive named 'Newcastle United' shown here approaching Newcastle Central Station in 1936 en-route to London from Edinburgh.

1972 marked the 80th anniversary of Newcastle United and this was part of the Football League Commemorative Series, issued on 11th November 1982.

Newcastle United and Liverpool contested the 1974 FA Cup Final at Wembley. Painfully, the match result is listed. The match comes under the special events category.

Ayresome Park, Middlesbrough hosted the 1974/75 Division One fixture between the previous season's Division Two Champions and FA Cup Finalists Newcastle United. It turned out not to be a match for the purists!

United played their one and only League Cup Final back in 1976 and were only beaten by a 'one in a million' goal from City's Dennis Tueart.

The two United's of Newcastle and Manchester clashed at St. James' Park and this match was part of the 'Live on TV Series' (ITV's 'The Match'). There were no goals for the viewers to enjoy though!

At the start of the 1992/93 season United opened their campaign with 11 straight wins, a club record. The 11th game was 2-1 derby day win at Roker Park, best remembered for Liam O'Brien's fabulous free-kick.

United's last game of the 1993/94 season, against Arsenal, marked Andy Cole's club record of 41 goals in a season for the club.

Having been runners-up in the Premier League in the 1995/96 season, United were invited to take part in the Charity Shield at Wembley the following August as Manchester United had won the double. The Red Devils won 4-0!

The 1998 FA Cup semi-final saw United defeat Sheffield United 1-0 at Old Trafford with Alan Shearer scoring the only goal of the game. This was part of the historical football series and included a stamp of Princess Diana.

Other popular items to collect are match tickets. Nowadays most games are all-ticket, so having a ticket isn't a particularly rare thing, but in times gone by, a big match ticket was a good item to have in your possession.

Here we display five tickets from United's last five visits to Wembley Stadium.

- FA Cup Final ticket from 1974
- League Cup Final ticket from 1976
- FA Charity Shield ticket from 1996
- FA Cup Final ticket from 1998
- FA Cup Final ticket from 1999

United fans will probably know that sadly United lost all five of those matches and only scored one goal in the process, Alan Gowling's consolation in the 1976 League Cup Final.

And an aside, United's FA Cup victory over Aston Villa at Wembley in 1924, only the second Cup Final to be played at the new National Stadium, was the first game to be designated as an all-ticket fixture (1924 ticket illustrated right). The reason being too many people, i.e. over the 100,000 capacity, tried to cram into Wembley for the 1923 Final between Bolton and West Ham.

UNITED IN THE COMMUNITY

Newcastle United Foundation, which has just celebrated its tenth year, is the official charity of Newcastle United Football Club. It uses the local passion for football to inspire, encourage learning and promote healthy lifestyles, making a real difference to the lives of children, young people and families in the North East region.

Through its health, community education and coaching programmes, the Foundation has worked with almost 50,000 people across Newcastle, Gateshead, North Tyneside and Northumberland in the last year. Here are a few pictures of some of the projects from last season, together with a number of other activities and events which the manager and players were involved with as part of their commitment to support the local community.

2

1 YEDLIN SURPRISES IVY ROAD PRIMARY SCHOOL PUPILS

Magpies defender DeAndre Yedlin visited pupils from Ivy Road Primary School who were taking part in a Tesco Bank Junior Players session led by Newcastle United Foundation.

Yedlin took the time to join in with session, which is a flagship community programme encouraging over 15,000 children in the North East to take part in physical activity each year.

2 GAYLE ANNOUNCED AS FOUNDATION DISABILITY PATRON

Newcastle United Foundation announced Dwight Gayle as their Ambassador for Disability Football at the start of the 2017/18 season.

Dwight approached the Foundation to determine how he could support their work with disabled children and has since met their Powerchair, DS Active and visually impaired players. The Foundation works with more than 2,378 participants on disability projects every year.

3 FOUNDATION DINNER

Newcastle United Foundation's 125 Years United fundraising dinner raised an incredible £47,000 for the charity.

The black tie event, hosted by Gabby Logan, saw Newcastle United Manager Rafa Benítez,

1

3

alongside current and former players, join together to support the achievements of Foundation participants as well as celebrating the Club's special anniversary.

The event also saw the Foundation launch their Project Pitchside capital appeal which will see them build a sports, education and wellbeing community hub on land close to St. James' Park.

4 HAYDEN SUPPORTS GIRLS FOOTBALL

Newcastle United Foundation had almost 1,000 girls involved in its Women and Girls football programmes in the last year. Ahead of the FA's Girls' Football Week, Isaac Hayden helped showcase the Foundation's girls football pathway on a feature for BBC's Match of the Day, which saw 100 girls invited to take part in a special training session, led by female coaches, at the First Team Training HQ.

5 MERINO IS A SUPER MOVER

Mikel Merino attended Choppington Primary School in Northumberland to help launch the new BBC Super Movers campaign. The initiative is a joint effort by the Premier League and the BBC to help primary school teachers inspire children to get more active. Merino was joined by CBBC stars Annabelle Davis and Miles Butler-Hughton, who led the children through various activities.

6 PREMIER LEAGUE PRIMARY STARS

Winners of the regional heats of the Premier League Primary Stars Competition, organised by Newcastle United Foundation, had an exciting week that culminated with a visit from Rafa Benítez at the first team training ground for the finals.

The Foundation works with more than 24,000 pupils per year across Newcastle, Gateshead, North Tyneside and Northumberland through Premier League Primary Stars. Schools involved enjoy some exclusive opportunities including player visits, the Premier League Trophy at their school, invitations to tournaments and signed NUFC memorabilia.

7

8

7 FOUNDATION 1892 CUP

At the start of the 2017/18 season the second Foundation 1892 Cup took place at the Newcastle United Academy. Established by Rafa Benítez the year before, 128 primary school pupils were once again invited to play in the tournament where they were presented with brand new kit to wear and take home, as well as enjoy a much deserved BBQ after the trophy presentations by Rafa. Cambois Primary School were the mixed teams winners while Walkergate Community School won the girls' tournament.

8 FOUNDATION ANNIVERSARY

Newcastle United Foundation celebrated its 10 year anniversary at the House of Lords in March 2018.

A number of high profile guests were in attendance including representatives from the Premier League, Foundation Trustee Steve Harper, and Patron Shola Ameobi.

The event celebrated a decade since the Foundation began helping disadvantaged young people in the North East – raising more than £13.5m over the last 10 years.

9 HOSPITALS

The visit to the local Newcastle hospitals in December is one of the highlights of the year for both the United players and staff as well as the children they meet whilst visiting the wards where they aim to bring some festive cheer to the children who are unfortunate enough to be hospitalised at this time of year. The Royal Victoria Infirmary, which houses the The Great North Children's Hospital, is the main beneficiary of the visit and they also receive a cash donation from the players.

10 MEET THE TEAM AT ST. JAMES' PARK

Signing sessions are always very popular events at Newcastle United, whether they are held at the Open Day, Christmas party or specially arranged sessions arranged for members or Junior Magpies.

Pictured here in United's Bar 1892 at St. James' Park are Jonjo Shelvey, Isaac Hayden and Karl Darlow.

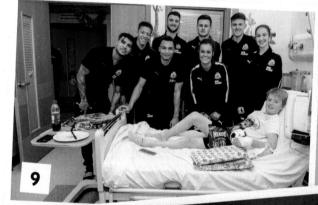

9

10

WORDSEARCH

Tackle the clues and find the answers in the grid. Names can go horizontally, vertically and diagonally in all eight directions. All 20 names are foreign players who have represented Newcastle United.

ANSWERS ON PAGE 62

U	O	I	L	I	S	A	V	A	P	A	P	M	K	Z
P	S	L	I	M	A	N	I	F	T	T	R	U	H	R
V	T	P	N	Q	N	X	P	J	R	L	C	D	R	R
E	S	S	I	C	K	Q	F	E	K	O	W	L	B	R
N	V	V	C	L	Y	N	B	D	L	Y	V	A	Q	O
F	G	A	M	J	U	L	T	O	T	H	I	N	K	D
K	K	S	R	A	A	A	C	N	B	C	D	J	M	E
M	N	P	N	D	R	C	L	E	D	U	U	I	V	L
N	N	R	J	I	I	T	Y	U	Q	B	K	W	A	B
A	A	I	Z	N	L	E	I	F	A	U	A	N	W	O
L	M	L	I	E	T	D	K	N	P	D	A	M	C	R
I	A	L	R	K	R	N	E	L	S	I	Q	M	B	K
V	H	A	D	L	N	M	M	Y	V	K	Z	K	R	L
A	V	T	J	L	O	V	E	N	K	R	A	N	D	S
G	M	I	R	A	N	D	I	N	H	A	N	N	H	Q

Cup Final scorer from 1952 (7)	**On loan from Leicester last season (7)**
The Belgium Prince (6)	**Nigerian centre-forward (7)**
Our first Brazilian (10)	**Australian goalscorer (6)**
DR Congo brothers (6)	**Club captain in 2013/14 (9)**
Colombian striker (7)	**Cypriot midfielder from 1993 (12)**
Senegalese right-back (4)	**Dutchman at Anfield (9)**
Signed from Hoffenheim in 2012 (5)	**American full-back (6)**
Turkish midfielder (4)	**Dane now at Rangers (11)**
Defender signed from Lille (7)	**Paraguayan winger (7)**
Portugal midfielder (5)	**German International (6)**

THE BEST GOALS
OF 2017/18

CHRISTIAN ATSU
v STOKE CITY
at ST. JAMES' PARK, 16TH SEPTEMBER 2017

United had won their last two games and this strike from Christian Atsu, his first Premier League goal, and his sixth for the club in all competitions, set them on their way to nine points out of nine and fourth place in the league. Atsu's strike was a clinical close range volley at the Leazes End past Jack Butland, after Isaac Hayden set up Matt Ritchie who put over a perfect cross from the right flank.

ISAAC HAYDEN v
SOUTHAMPTON at
ST MARY'S STADIUM, 15TH OCTOBER 2017

Just likè his goal at the end of the 2016/17 season at Cardiff, this was a fine strike from outside the box and, like Christian Atsu, his first Premier League goal. With 20 minutes on the clock, Atsu's goalbound effort rebounded for Isaac Hayden to fire a low 20-yarder beyond former Magpie Fraser Forster who was caught flat-footed in front of the wildly celebrating Geordie hordes behind the goal.

HENRI SAIVET v WEST HAM at THE LONDON STADIUM, 23RD DECEMBER 2017

Henri Saivet, making his first appearance of the season, had just gifted West Ham their opening goal. But then, a foul on Christian Atsu to the left hand side of the box saw play pulled back for a free kick. Saivet stepped up and hit a superb curling right footed free-kick from 25 yards, beating Adrian low at his near post. The Spanish custodian was possibly expecting a cross rather than a shot, but the kick was well-placed and hit with great power.

MO DIAMÉ v WEST HAM at THE LONDON STADIUM, 23RD DECEMBER 2017

Just after the break United sprung forward to take a 2-1 lead in this crucial encounter at the wrong end of the table. Ciaran Clark played a measured pass out to Christian Atsu down the Newcastle left and after he outwitted Pablo Zabaleta, he crossed for Mo Diamé to hammer a right-footed effort into the top corner from eight yards out. Keeper Adrián had no chance whatsoever as the ball was past him before he could react.

AYOZE PÉREZ v STOKE CITY at THE BET365 STADIUM, 1ST JANUARY 2018

United were sat in 16th place in the League and with Stoke just one point above them, this was a vital game for both teams. Charlie Adam lost the ball in midfield which allowed Jacob Murphy to push on. With space opening up ahead of him, he crossed into the opposition half before swinging over a low centre towards the unmarked Ayoze Pérez. The Tenerife front-man flicked it right-footed into the net from six yards via the boot of goalkeeper Jack Butland. Classic Ayoze.

JACOB MURPHY v MANCHESTER CITY at THE ETIHAD STADIUM, 20TH JANUARY 2018

Not many away teams scored at the Etihad last season and less still put the hosts under any sort of pressure. United did both, albeit for a brief period before City sealed their win with a third. Ciaran Clark gathered a loose ball and sent Jacob Murphy through on goal, running at pace. His dink over Ederson was sublime as he found the back of the net before retrieving the ball and acknowledging the celebrating away fans as he headed back to the halfway line.

MATT RITCHIE v MANCHESTER UNITED at ST. JAMES' PARK, 11TH FEBRUARY 2018

A huge win for United. Visiting defender Chris Smalling was booked for a dive inside his own half when there was no contact from Jonjo Shelvey and fittingly it was Jonjo who delivered the free kick that Florian Lejeune headed across the box. Dwight Gayle adroitly flicked the ball into the path of Matt Ritchie who picked his spot with a first time left-footed effort into the Leazes net to the left of David de Gea, sending home fans wild with delight.

KENEDY v SOUTHAMPTON at ST. JAMES' PARK, 10TH MARCH 2018

The first goals scored by United's Brazilian loanee. Jonjo Shelvey's forward pass just over a minute into the game reached Kenedy as his run took him into the Southampton box. He took it on his chest, turning adeptly before hitting his shot into the turf and over Alex McCarthy into the Leazes End net. And what's more, a second Kenedy goal arrived before the half hour, a superb breakaway strike. The man from Chelsea certainly made a big impact on Tyneside.

AYOZE PÉREZ v HUDDERSFIELD TOWN at ST. JAMES' PARK, 31ST MARCH 2018

Ayoze Pérez took the ball out of his half and played it wide to Christian Atsu. The winger beat his man and crossed to the far post where Islam Slimani was waiting to head home, but was denied by keeper Jonas Lössl who managed to palm the ball away. Fortunately it fell to Kenedy and the Brazilian had the presence of mind to pick out the unmarked Ayoze Pérez who slotted home from six yards amid great acclaim.

AYOZE PÉREZ v LEICESTER CITY at THE KING POWER STADIUM, 7TH APRIL 2018

This was a win that took United to the verge of survival. Florian Lejeune played the ball forward over halfway towards Ayoze Pérez and when the home defensive pair of Harry Maguire and Wes Morgan left it for each other, Pérez took advantage to perfectly clip the ball over Kasper Schmeichel with the outside of his right foot, the ball bouncing on the goal line and into the back of the net. The identity of the goalkeeper drew comparisons with the famous Philippe Albert lob over Kasper's father Peter back in October 1996.

MATT RITCHIE v ARSENAL at ST. JAMES' PARK, 15TH APRIL 2018

Paul Dummett's throw in down the United left was directed to Islam Slimani, but he was out jumped by Mustafi. His clearing header dropped to Nacho Monreal and he in turn aimlessly headed it on. Enter substitute Slimani who attacked the ball and headed it strongly infield and across the box. A deft touch from Pérez helped it on to Matt Ritchie, who was beyond Rob Holding and able to coolly pass it into the Gallowgate goal before demolishing the corner flag in typical fashion.

FROM THE ARCHIVES

A classic picture from the 1980s as fans queue for tickets from the old box office. The West Stand is in the background together with one of the four towering floodlight pylons in the south west corner of the Gallowgate End.

Two United legends pictured before a game in 1952, Chilean George Robledo on the left scored 91 goals in 166 games for the Magpies whilst Geordie number line legend Jackie Milburn notched 200 goals in his 397 games for the club. What a partnership they were!

United stars past and present from 1982 including a young Paul Gascoigne in the middle of the front row. Terry McDermott is front row far left, Mick Martin, far right and in the back row, Jeff Clarke is third from the left, David McCreery third right and Colin Suggett far right.

Players from the early 1950s pass the time enjoying a game of cards, still a popular pastime today on the coach to away games. Pictured left to right are Bobby Mitchell, Charlie Crowe, Bobby Cowell, Ronnie Simpson and Duggie Livingstone. Mitchell and Cowell both played in all three FA Cup wins in 1951, 1952 and 1955.

The famous Gallowgate End in 1969 with the old scoreboard, invaluable for getting half time and full time scores, at the back of the terrace. In those days the Leazes End was still 'the end' for United's most boisterous and noisy supporters.

Willie McFaul and Tommy Cassidy relax on deck chairs at the Selsdon Park Hotel in Surrey in May 1974 prior to the FA Cup Final at Wembley. Sadly United never got going at Wembley either, losing 3-0 to a Kevin Keegan inspired Liverpool.

St. James' Park action from season 1973/74. Leicester City are the visitors in a 1-1 draw. England goalkeeper Peter Shilton, in an unusual all white strip, punches clear from United's Keith Robson with David Craig (left) and Terry McDermott looking on.

Alan Shearer leads United out in a Champions League group stage tie against Inter Milan in the San Siro in March 2003. United's number nine scored both goals in a 2-2 draw in a match best remembered for the huge following of Geordies in Milan, over 10,000 having made the trip to Italy's fashion capital.

St. James' Park in 1972 and it's an empty Popular Terrace as the backdrop for this picture for the game against Tottenham Hotspur. The reason? Well the new East Stand, still in place today, was being constructed which would open in January 1973. And for the record, Irving Nattrass (number 4) is scoring United's third against the Londoners.

Wembley 1976 and the United squad are in London the day before the League Cup Final against Manchester City. It was traditional in those days for the players to visit the stadium the day before the game just to acquaint themselves with the surroundings. Pictured left to right are Glenn Keeley, Ray Blackhall, Paul Cannell, Micky Burns, Stewart Barrowclough and Alan Gowling, who would go on to score at the famous old stadium in United's 2-1 defeat.

ICELAND

NEWCASTLE UNITED IN EUROPE

Newcastle United have a rich history in European football having played the seventh highest number of games in terms of English clubs in Europe (134) and of course the Magpies lifted the Inter-Cities Fairs Cup (now the Europa League) back in 1969, led by captain Bob Moncur, in what was their first taste of European football. This map illustrates the 63 different teams United have met on their travels and the 27 different countries the black 'n' whites have played games in.

Where a number appears in brackets, e.g. Barcelona (2), it indicates the teams have met twice in Europe, either home and away over two legs or home and away in a group. Countries coloured in grey indicate where United have yet to play.

Belgium
1. Club Brugge
2. RSC Anderlecht
3. Royal Antwerp
4. Sporting Lokeren
5. Zulte Waregem

Bosnia
6. Zeljeznicar

Bulgaria
7. CSKA Sofia

Croatia
8. Croatia Zagreb

England
9. Southampton

Estonia
10. Levadia Tallinn

France
11. Bordeaux
12. Marseille
13. Metz
14. Monaco
15. SEC Bastia
16. Sochaux
17. Troyes

Germany
18. Bayer Leverkusen
19. Eintracht Frankfurt
20. 1860 Munich

Georgia
21. Dinamo Tbilisi

Greece
22. Atromitos
23. Olympiacos
24. Panionios

Holland
25. AZ Alkmaar
26. Feyenoord
27. Heerenveen
28. NAC Breda
29. PSV Eindhoven (2)

Hungary
30. Ferencvaros
31. Pecsi Dozsa
32. Ujpest Dozsa

Italy
33. Internazionale (2)
34. Juventus
35. Palermo
36. Roma

Israel
37. Hapoel Sakhnin

Latvia
38. FK Ventspils

Norway
39. Lillestrom
40. Valerenga IF

Portugal
41. Benfica
42. Maritimo
43. Porto
44. Sporting Lisbon (3)
45. Vitoria Setubal

Republic of Ireland
46. Bohemians

Russia
47. Anzhi Makhachkala

Scotland
48. Dundee United
49. Rangers

Serbia
50. Partizan Belgrade (2)

Slovakia
51. Dubnica

Spain
52. Athletic Bilbao
53. Barcelona (2)
54. Celta Vigo
55. Deportivo La Coruna
56. Real Mallorca
57. Real Zaragoza

Sweden
58. Halmstads

Switzerland
59. FC Basel
60. FC Zurich

Turkey
61. Fenerbahce

Ukraine
62. Dynamo Kiev (2)
63. Metalist Kharkiv

48

49

IRELAND 46

U.K.

9

55

54

43

45

PORTUGAL

SPA

41 44

42

A TO Z OF UNITED

ARSENAL – The Magpies have played the Gunners more times than any other club, a record 180 occasions.

BRAZIL – Three Samba footballers have represented United in the Premier League era; Fumaça, Caçapa and, most recently, Kenedy (below).

CAMBRIDGE – when United lost 1-0 at Cambridge in 1984, it ended the host's 31 match run without a victory – the league's worst ever winless run!

DAVIES – Three United players called Davies – Reg, Ian and Alan – coincidentally also played for Carlisle and Swansea.

EVERTON – United's heaviest ever half-time deficit was recorded at Goodison Park (below) in October 1931. The Magpies were 6-0 down at the interval, going on to lose 8-1.

FULHAM – When United lost 3-2 at Craven Cottage in September 1934, they found themselves bottom of Division Two for the first time in their history.

GRIMSBY – The first ever own goal scored by a United player, Tom Rodger, was recorded in favour of the Mariners in 1894.

HOLLINS – Dave played for United and when brother John lined up for Chelsea against the Magpies in 1965, the two brothers were made captains for the day.

IPSWICH – Town's George Burley scored the fastest-ever own goal seen at St. James' Park after just 20 seconds, as his side were defeated 3-0 by United in 1984.

JINKY – Jimmy 'Jinky' Smith (above) was United's midfield 'entertainer' in the early 1970s.

KICK OFF – Lord Beresford, Admiral of the Fleet, kicked off this Tyne-Wear derby friendly fixture in 1904 (below).

L EE – Rob is the last man to score at Wembley for United, back in 2000, in the FA Cup Semi Final against Chelsea (above).

M ANCHESTER CITY – Jackie Milburn scored United's 3000th League goal when he netted against the Sky Blues in September 1949.

N 'ZOGBIA – Charles, the only player in the Premier League era (other than the three O'Brien's) to have an apostrophe after the first letter of his surname

O RIENT – United's first opponents on BBC Match of the Day in February 1965.

P LYMOUTH – The Pilgrims' Home Park ground (below) was the venue where United clinched the Championship title in 2010.

Q UINTESSENTIAL – Sir Bobby Robson, representing the most perfect example of quality and class as United manager.

R OCHDALE – The Dale are one of only seven league clubs still to face United in competitive football.

S CUNTHORPE – The Iron were United's first League Cup victims, losing 2-0 at Newcastle in September 1961.

T RAINING – A bit different over 100 years ago, Jimmy Howie and Jack Carr (below), both Edwardian legends.

U NUSED – Last season Javier Manquillo was United's most unused substitute, remaining on the bench on 17 occasions.

V EITCH – The Edwardian legend (above) died at the relatively young age of 56 in Bern, Switzerland on the opening day of the 1938/39 season.

W HITE – Yorkshireman Len is United's third highest goalscorer with 153 strikes for the Magpies.

X UEREB – Ray, the Maltese International almost signed for United in 1977 after impressing after a one month trial.

Y ORK CITY –United striker Arthur Bottom scored more goals for York in one season (31) than any other player before transferring to United in 1958.

Z ICO – Not the Brazilian World Cup star from 1982 but Mick Martin, club captain in the late 1970s and affectionately known as Zico.

NUMBER 9 HEROES

Tyneside loves its hero figures. Newcastle United's history has been packed with a colourful collection of larger than life personalities who have pulled on the black n' white shirt; characters who have caught the imagination of the club's fanatical support. And none more so than those in the famous Number 9 shirt.

Bill Appleyard

Jock Peddie

Albert Shepherd

Willie Thompson

The centre-forward role at St. James' Park is now a legendary tale. For a century a whole line of famous centre-forwards have donned the black n' white colours and continually stirred the Geordie crowd. Many dashing, courageous and dynamic players almost out of the Roy of the Rovers comic strip. Each a Geordie hero.

While former United and England skipper and £15m centre-forward Alan Shearer remains the most recent hero, over one hundred years ago pioneer Willie Thompson was the first to play in the centre-forward role. Sporting a monster moustache in the fashion of the day, the Northumbrian hit plenty of goals as Newcastle became established as a Football League

club. But it was the signing of Glasgow born Jock Peddie that marked the arrival of the Club's first hero figure. The tough Scot arrived on Tyneside late in 1897 from Third Lanark with a reputation for being a free scoring, tearaway leader with a blockbuster shot in either foot. He was big and strong and netted 78 goals during a five year stay at Gallowgate.

Next to hold the number nine mantle was Bill Appleyard, a 14 stone terror to goalkeepers. He arrived in April 1903 from Grimsby Town where he had also worked as a North Sea fisherman. A superb goal poacher, especially on the right flank, he also aimed to put the goalkeeper in the net as well as the ball! Bill scored 88 goals in 146 games and won Championship and FA Cup medals, only narrowly missing an international call-up for England. Injury sadly curtailed his career so United plunged into the transfer market in a big way and brought Albert Shepherd to Tyneside in

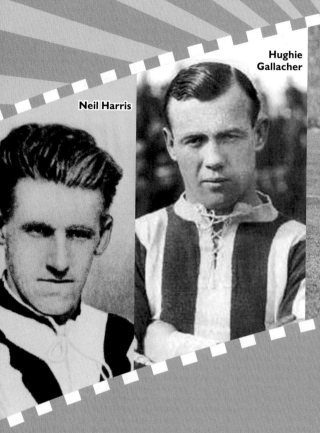

Neil Harris

Hughie Gallacher

Jack Allen

Albert Stubbins

November 1908 and he immediately became a hit with the fans. He was noted for his exciting dashes through the middle and averaged over a goal every second game for the Magpies, scoring 92 in five seasons.

Like Appleyard, Albert Shepherd won title and cup honours before an injury halted his progress. And by the time Newcastle were ready to start football after the First World War, they needed a new figure to raise the pulse rate on the terraces. That man was Neil Harris who joined the club in May 1920 from Partick Thistle. At his peak in 1924, the Scot netted in United's FA Cup victory at Wembley and also led his country's line against England.

Next up the black n' whites set their sights on a five foot five bundle of magic from north of the border who was to become perhaps the greatest figure to appear in a United shirt. Hughie Gallacher joined the Tynesiders in December 1925 for £6,500, a record fee, and is ranked alongside Everton legend Dixie Dean as the greatest striker of them all.

Hughie could shoot powerfully, head, dribble, create openings, tackle, forage, run all day and often got into trouble with defenders, referees and directors! Goalscoring came naturally. He scored 463 goals at senior level and accumulated 143 for United in only 174 games.

Newcastle never really found a replacement for Gallacher, not until Albert Stubbins came along just before the war. Several players gave supporters something to cheer in between, including Jack Allen, a local product from Newburn who scored 41 goals in a short but productive stay, including two goals in the 1932 FA Cup final. Wallsend born Stubbins was the nations top striker during wartime football and grabbed a staggering 237 goals in only 218 games for the Magpies before moving to Liverpool in 1946. Charlie Wayman then took the No 9 shirt for a season before Jackie Milburn was a reluctant replacement. Wor Jackie never wanted to play in the centre-forward's role, but manager George Martin persuaded the former Ashington pit-lad to have a go. And of course he was an instant success.

For the next decade, and for many years after he had left St. James' Park, Milburn was the fans' darling. Jackie's name immediately revives memories of one of the most exciting and thrilling eras in the club's history – lifting the

Len White

Ron McGarry

Wyn Davies

Peter Withe

Mirandinha

Micky Quinn

FA Cup three times in five years. In almost 500 games for the Magpies, Jackie netted 239 goals (including war-time football). It is the best on record by any player connected with the Magpies and it wasn't so much the huge number of goals he scored, as the breathtaking manner in which he scored them.

Jackie departed in 1957 and Newcastle had a readymade replacement to step into both the goalscoring and heroes shoes, Len White, a Yorkshire miner, who netted 153 goals in 270 fixtures with a style that enthralled the fans.

Newcastle's period in the Second Division saw Barrie Thomas and Ron McGarry take over the crowd's mantle and the No 9 shirt. Both were characters and Thomas can also claim to have an excellent return of goals – 50 in 78 matches.

The Geordie crowd soon found a new idol though as flame haired Welshman Wyn Davies arrived at Gallowgate in 1966 and his contribution to the club winning European silverware was enormous. The Mighty Wyn was as tough as they come, and able to soak up many a severe physical battering from defenders whilst being the perfect target man.

The end of the Davies era came in 1971 and that year saw the beginning of another classic period when another No 9 of special star quality landed on Tyneside. A brash, arrogant 21 year old, Malcolm Macdonald pulled up at St. James' Park in a Rolls Royce. His style of play provided United's supporters with thrill-a-minute action. Macdonald was lightning fast, he had a cracking shot, was strong as a mule and deceivingly good in the air too.

Supermac's departure was a blow and United found it hard to replace his powerplay at centre-forward and they didn't really do so until Peter Withe, Mick Quinn and Andy Cole arrived several years later. The fans affection was heaped upon a certain Kevin Keegan in the intervening years, one of United's few non centre-forward hero figures.

Once Keegan had departed, Brazilian international centre-forward Mirandinha settled on Tyneside with a big reputation, but failed to live up to the headlines.

Dwight Gayle

Obafemi Martins

Alan Shearer

Les Ferdinand

Papiss Cisse

Andy Cole

Andy Carroll

Then a chirpy scouser by the name of Mick Quinn was signed by manager Jim Smith in 1989. The former Portsmouth striker got off to a marvellous start – the best by any United centre-forward. He netted four goals on his debut against Leeds United and the Mighty Quinn had arrived.

Kevin Keegan then brought Andy Cole to Tyneside and what a predator he was. A total of 68 goals in 84 appearances ensured that the lithe striker became a huge hit with the Geordie public. He broke the club's individual scoring record in season 1993-94 with 41 goals.

Cole left for Old Trafford and The Toon Army had to wait until the £6m signing of Les Ferdinand in 1995 before their much needed hero figure had reappeared. Sir Les immediately took to the role and found the best form of his career as Newcastle challenged for the title in 1995/96.

Then, the return of Alan Shearer in 1996 to the club he supported as a kid – for a world record £15m fee

– was just what the Toon Army longed for. If it wasn't a centre-forward hero they loved, it was a local lad made good – Shearer was both. His all round game and professional attitude ensured he became the perfect North East ambassador and probably United's greatest No 9 Hero of All-Time.

Nigerian Obafemi Martins took the number nine mantle briefly between 2006 and 2009 before homegrown Geordie youngster Andy Carroll grabbed the shirt with great aplomb for the 2010/11 season before January 2012 transfer window signing Papiss Cissé hit a sensational 13 goals in 14 games in the remaining months of that season. And now, right up to date, the Number 9 shirt has been worn by Dwight Gayle for the past two seasons.

QUIZ ANSWERS

Page 19

Page 39

Current

1) Chelsea
2) Islam Slimani
3) Kenedy
4) Burnley
5) Christian Atsu
6) Stoke and West Ham
7) 51,992
8) Simon Smith
9) Hellas Verona
10) Dele Alli

Old

1) Parma (Italy)
2) Rob Lee
3) Edgar (Eddie and David)
4) 1910
5) 34
6) 3-2 to Newcastle
7) Jackie Milburn (23)
8) Arsenal
9) Kevin Nolan
10) Peterborough

Page 27

Page 47

U	O	I	L	I	S	A	V	A	P	A	P	M	K	Z
P	S	L	I	M	A	N	I	F	T	T	R	U	H	R
V	T	P	N	Q	N	X	P	J	R	L	C	D	R	R
E	S	S	I	C	K	Q	F	E	K	O	W	L	B	R
N	V	V	C	L	Y	N	B	D	L	Y	V	A	Q	O
F	G	A	M	J	U	L	T	O	T	H	I	N	K	D
K	K	S	R	A	A	A	C	N	B	C	D	J	M	E
M	N	P	N	D	R	C	L	E	D	U	U	I	V	L
N	N	R	J	I	I	T	Y	U	Q	B	K	W	A	B
A	A	I	Z	N	L	E	I	F	A	U	A	N	W	O
L	M	L	I	E	T	D	K	N	P	D	A	M	C	R
I	A	L	R	K	R	N	E	L	S	I	Q	M	B	K
V	H	A	D	L	N	M	M	Y	V	K	Z	K	R	L
A	V	T	J	L	O	V	E	N	K	R	A	N	D	S
G	M	I	R	A	N	D	I	N	H	A	N	N	H	Q

Cup Final scorer from 1952 (7) = Robledo
On loan from Leicester last season (7) = Slimani
The Belgium Prince (6) = Albert
Nigerian centre-forward (7) = Martins
Our first Brazilian (10) = Mirandinha
Australian goalscorer (6) = Viduka
DR Congo brothers (6) = LuaLua
Club captain in 2013/14 (9) = Coloccini
Colombian striker (7) = Asprilla
Cypriot midfielder from 1993 (12) = Papavasiliou
Senegalese right-back (4) = Beye
Dutchman at Anfield (9) = Wijnaldum
Signed from Hoffenheim in 2012 (5) = Cisse
American full-back (6) = Yedlin
Turkish midfielder (4) = Emre
Dane now at Rangers (11) = Lovenkrands
Defender signed from Lille (7) = Dubuchy
Paraguayan winger (7) = Gavilan
Portugal midfielder (5) = Viana
German International (6) = Hamann